An Elementary Study of Islam

About The Author

Ḥaḍrat Mirza Tahir Ahmad (1928–2003), may Allah have infinite mercy on his soul, a man of God, Voice articulate of the age, a great orator, a deeply learned scholar of phenomenal intelligence, a prolific and versatile writer, a keen student of comparative religions was loved and devoutly followed by his more than 10 million Ahmadi Muslim followers all over the world as their Imam, the spiritual head, being the fourth successor of Ḥaḍrat Mirza Ghulam Ahmad (the Promised Messiah and Mahdi[as]), to which august office he was elected as Khalīfatul Masīḥ in 1982.

After the promulgation of general Zia-ul-Haq anti-Ahmadiyya Ordinance of 26th April 1984 he had to leave his beloved country, Pakistan, and migrated to England from where he launched Muslim Television Ahmadiyya International (MTA) which would (and still does) telecast its programmes 24 hours a day to the four corners of the world.

Besides being a religious leader, he was a homeopathic physician of world fame, a highly gifted poet and a sportsman.

He had his schooling in Qadian, India, and later joined the Govt. College, Lahore, Pakistan, and after graduating from Jāmi'ah Ahmadiyya, Rabwah, Pakistan with distinction, he obtained his honours degree in Arabic from the Punjab University, Lahore. From 1955 to 1957 he studied at the School of Oriental and African Studies, University of London.

He had a divinely inspired and very deep knowledge of the Holy Quran which he translated into Urdu. He also partially revised and added explanatory notes to the English translation of the Holy Quran by Ḥaḍrat Maulawī Sher Ali[ra]. *Revelation, Rationality, Knowledge and Truth* is his magnum opus.

Though he had no formal education in philosophy and science, he had a philosophical bent of mind and tackled most difficult and abstruse theological-philosophical questions with great acumen and ease and his intellectual approach was always rational and scientific. For a layman he had an amazingly in-depth knowledge of science, especially life sciences which attracted him most. He also had deep knowledge of human psychology. His was an analytical mind of high intelligence—an intellect scintillating with brilliance, capable of solving knottiest problems with ease, leaving his listeners and readers spellbound.

An Elementary Study of Islam

Mirza Tahir Ahmad

Islam International Publications Ltd.
Tilford, Surrey

An Elementary Study of Islam
by Mirza Tahir Ahmad

© Islam International Publications Ltd.

First published in English in 1985
Reprinted in 1997, 2003, 2010, 2015
Present reprint (USA) 2017

Published by
Ahmadiyya Muslim Community, USA
15000 Good Hope Road
Silver Spring, MD 20905 USA
www.trueislam.com
1-800-949-4752 (1-800-Why-Islam)

Cover design by Salman Muhammad Sajid
Book layout by Dr. Abdul Majid Shah & Masood Nasir
Index prepared by Dr. Abdul Majid Shah & Salman Muhammad Sajid

ISBN: 1 85372 562 5
10 9 8 7 6

Contents

Publisher's Note

According to our system of counting Quranic verses, the verse *Bismillāh irraḥmān irraḥīm* (In the name of Allah, the Most Gracious, Ever Merciful) is counted as the first verse of the chapter, which it precedes. Some publishers of the Holy Quran however, begin counting following *Bismillāh irraḥmān irraḥīm*. Should the reader not find the relevant verse under the number mentioned in this book, he or she is advised to deduct 1 from the number. For example, if this book quotes *Surah Al-Faṭir (35:25)*, then some copies of the Holy Quran will list the same verse under *Surah Al-Faṭir (35: 24)*.

Where necessary, translation of the Arabic text has been elaborated by additional words to explain the meaning. Such words are not in italics. The word *and* at the commencement of a translated verse has been omitted.

The form *ibn* has been used in both initial and medial position in the names of persons, in order to conform to current usage, although *bin* also occurs medially in some original texts (abbreviated usually as *b.*).

Quotations from the Holy Bible are from the New World Translation.

The name of Muhammad[sa], the Holy Prophet of Islam, has been followed by the symbol [sa], which is an abbreviation for the prayer (ﷺ) *Ṣallallāhu 'Alaihi Wasallam* (may peace and blessings of Allah be upon him). The names of other Prophets[as] and messengers are followed by the symbol [as], an abbreviation for (عليه السلام/عليهم السلام) *'Alaihissalām/'Alaihimussalām* (on whom be peace). The actual prayers have not generally been set out in full, but they should nevertheless, be understood as being repeated in full in each case. The symbol [ra] is used with the name of the Companions of the Holy Prophet[sa] and those of the Promised Messiah[as]. It stands for (رضي الله عنه/عنها/عنهم) *Raḍī Allāhu 'anhu/'anhā/'anhum* (may Allah be pleased with him/with her/with them). [rh] stands for (رحمه الله) *Raḥimahullāhu Ta'ālā* (may Allah's blessing be on him). [at] stands for (ايده الله) *Ayyadahullāhu Ta'ālā* (may Allah, the Almighty help him).

In transliterating Arabic words we have followed the following system adopted by the Royal Asiatic Society:

ا	at the beginning of a word, pronounced as *a, i, u* preceded by a very slight aspiration, like *h* in the English word *honour*.
ث	*th,* pronounced like *th* in the English word *thing*.
ح	*ḥ,* a guttural aspirate, stronger than *h*.
خ	*kh,* pronounced like the Scotch *ch* in *loch*.
ذ	*dh,* pronounced like the English *th* in *that*.
ص	*ṣ,* strongly articulated *s*.
ض	*ḍ,* similar to the English *th* in *this*.
ط	*ṭ,* strongly articulated palatal *t*.
ظ	*ẓ,* strongly articulated *z*.
ع	*',* a strong guttural, the pronunciation of which must be learnt by the ear.

غ   *gh,* a sound approached very nearly in the r *grasseye* in French, and in the German *r.* It requires the muscles of the throat to be in the 'gargling' position whilst pronouncing it.

ق   *q,* a deep guttural *k* sound.

ئ   ', a sort of catch in the voice.

Short vowels are represented by:

a   for ——⸜—— (like *u* in *bud*)

i   for ———⸝— (like *i* in *bid*)

u   for ——ء—— (like *oo* in *wood*)

Long vowels by:

ā   for ——١—— or آ (like *a* in *father*);

ī   for ى ———⸝— or ———ا— (like *ee* in *deep*);

ū   for و ——ء—— (like *oo* in *root*);

Other:

ai   for ى ——⸜—— (like *i* in *site*)*;

au   for و ——⸜—— (resembling *ou* in *sound*)

Please note that in transliterated words the letter *e* is to be pronounced as in *prey* which rhymes with *day*; however the pronunciation is flat without the element of English diphthong. If in Urdu and Persian words *e* is lengthened a bit more, it is transliterated as *ei* to be pronounced as *ei* in *feign* without the element of diphthong.

---

*   In Arabic words like شیخ (Shaikh) there is an element of diphthong which is missing when the word is pronounced in Urdu.

Thus ـکـ is transliterated as *kei*. For the nasal sound of *n* we have used the symbol *ń*. Thus the Urdu word مین is transliterated as *meiń*.*

The consonants not included in the above list have the same phonetic value as in the principal languages of Europe.

We have not transliterated Arabic words which have become part of English language, e.g., Islam, Mahdi, Quran[†], Hijra, Ramadan, Hadith, ulama, umma, sunna, kafir, pukka, etc.

Curved commas are used in the system of transliteration, ' for ع, ' for ء. Commas as punctuation marks are used according to the normal usage. Similarly, normal usage is followed for the apostrophe.

---

*   These transliterations are not included in the system of transliteration by The Royal Asiatic Society.

†   Concise Oxford Dictionary records Quran in three forms—Quran, Qur'an and Koran.

Foreword

On March 12, 1990, at the invitation of the Department of Islamic Studies, Seville University, Spain, Hadhrat Mirza Tahir Ahmad[rh] delivered an address entitled *Islam—A Discourse on its Elementary and Fundamental Teachings*. He was advised by the Head of the Department to introduce Islam at an elementary level, keeping in view that most of the audience, drawn from other departments and the general public, would have very little knowledge of Islam. The time allotted for the speech was limited to one hour. He provided a brief introduction to the Islamic faith and touched upon a variety of very important topics. He showed how religious teachings have evolved over time culminating in the complete and universal teachings and emphasised the areas of similarities between Islam and other religions.

This treatise has been developed out of that speech. The author has expanded on various themes, which time didn't permit him in the original lecture. Additionally, in converting the spoken word into writing, certain changes and amendments were also effected by the speaker himself. In this book he highlighted the salient characteristics especially the universal nature of Islam which renders it capable of uniting the people from all the nations of the world under one banner of peace. The author brought this short treatise to a close, with an earnest appeal to the leadership of the world religions: *"The quest for peace is a matter of human survival, and as such should not be taken lightly."*

May Allah Almighty make this booklet a source of enlightenment and guidance to help understand the basic teachings of Islam for all. Ameen.

An Elementary
Study of Islam

أَشْهَدُ اَنْ لَّا اِلٰهَ اِلَّا اللّٰهُ وَحْدَهُ لَا شَرِيْكَ لَهُ وَ

أَشْهَدُ اَنَّ مُحَمَّدًا عَبْدُهُ وَ رَسُوْلُهُ

أَمَّا بَعْدُ فَاَعُوْذُ بِاللّٰهِ مِنَ الشَّيْطٰنِ الرَّجِيْمِ

بِسْمِ اللّٰهِ الرَّحْمٰنِ الرَّحِيْمِ ۝
اَلْحَمْدُ لِلّٰهِ رَبِّ الْعٰلَمِيْنَ ۝ الرَّحْمٰنِ الرَّحِيْمِ ۝
مٰلِكِ يَوْمِ الدِّيْنِ ۝
اِيَّاكَ نَعْبُدُ وَ اِيَّاكَ نَسْتَعِيْنُ ۝
اِهْدِنَا الصِّرَاطَ الْمُسْتَقِيْمَ ۝
صِرَاطَ الَّذِيْنَ اَنْعَمْتَ عَلَيْهِمْ ۙ
غَيْرِ الْمَغْضُوْبِ عَلَيْهِمْ وَلَا الضَّآلِّيْنَ ۝   *

After the traditional recitation and reciting the *Surah Al-Fātiḥa* (the opening chapter of the Holy Quran), the Head of Jamāʿat Ahmadiyya commenced as follows:

I consider it a singular honour that the Department of Islamic Studies, Scville University has thought it fit to invite me here this evening to address you on the fundamental teachings of Islam. Before I came, I was advised that I should speak on the basics of Islam so that the students who are not well versed in this subject and who have only an elementary knowledge should be able to understand. That surprised me indeed. It surprised me in the first place because I was expecting university students to have fared better. Secondly, I was surprised because Spain has a long history of contact with Islam. Yet for it to have lost that contact so completely as to have erased even the faintest impression, is astonishing indeed! Here I am today to introduce to you the basic teachings of Islam.

When I visited Spain in 1982 to inaugurate a mosque built by the Ahmadiyya Community, which incidentally was the first mosque to be built here after a break of five hundred years, many eyebrows were raised. During my press conference I was repeatedly confronted with the same questions as to why we should come to Spain. What was the purpose? Was there any sinister motive attached to this exercise? Haven't we had enough of Islam? Should we take it to be a new form of the invasion of Spain? My reply to all such questions was, 'Yes, I have come to invade Spain, but not with the intention of winning territories by the sword, but to win hearts with a message of love and persuasion.'

That reply still holds good. We as a community in Islam are not built on the same pattern as the commonly perceived image of Islam on the reflecting mirror of the so-called fundamentalists. Today therefore, I will endeavour to present Islam to you not with reference to the Muslim behaviour in different countries, but with reference only to the basic teachings of Islam found in the divine book, the Holy Quran, and the conduct and traditions of the Holy Founder[sa] of Islam.

Islam means *peace*. Therein lies the soul and spirit of Islam. It is ironic that this religion of peace is understood today in the West as the religion of war, terrorism, chaos and disorder. While in reality Islam is not only peace in name, but peace pervades all its teachings, and works as the key to its understanding. If translated literally, the second meaning of the word Islam is *submission*. So the words *peace* and *submission* create a complete picture of Islam. While peace is in relation to the Muslim's attitude to his fellow human beings and also in relation to the deep content he finds in Islam, the word submission describes the attitude of the Muslim to God. So in one single word, the entire philosophy of this religion is summed up. It is interesting to note that according to Islam, every true religion must have these two requisite features to indicate its divine origin. All religions, according to Islam, endeavoured to bring man back to his creator on the one hand, and to establish an ideal relationship with his fellow human beings on the other.

Islam has five fundamental articles of faith, which must be professed by everyone who desires to become a Muslim. Although Islam is already divided into many sects like all other religions, but on this issue there are no two opinions. By whatever title the sects are recognised, be they Sunnis or Shi'ites, all believe in these five fundamental articles.

* ❖ The first of these is to firmly believe in the absolute oneness of God . It is a Unity which is unsplittable and indivisible, and one which cannot be multiplied or compromised in any form.
* ❖ The second article relates to the belief in angels. Although there are varying opinions among Muslims about the concept of angels, nonetheless all Muslims believe in the existence of angels.

❖ The third article relates to belief in the books. The books in religious terms refer to such divine scriptures as contain new teachings and bring a new religious law. They are mentioned after the angels because most often revelation is transmitted to man through the agency of angels, who play a central role in carrying the divine message to the messengers. Angels have many other tasks to perform, but of that we will discuss later.

❖ The fourth article relates to the messengers or prophets, who sometimes bring a new code of life and a new law for a specific people in a specific age and who sometimes are sent only for the purpose of reform.

❖ The fifth and last article of faith relates to the Day of Judgement. It also implies that every human being will be raised after death in some form, and will be held answerable to God with regards to the life he had led here on earth.

These are the five fundamentals of Islam. However, according to some there is a sixth constituent of Muslim belief included in the fundamentals by the Holy Founder of Islam, and that is belief in Divine Decree. Let us now turn to a more detailed study of these articles one by one.

The Belief in the Unity of God

This seems to be a rather simple and elementary concept. It should not be difficult for anybody to understand the oneness of God, and there the matter seems to rest. But in fact there is far more to this than meets the eye. When one examines the concept of Unity in depth, the entire world of religion seems to revolve around this pivotal point. This belief influences man's life in all its aspects. It also implies the negation of all else but God. So belief in the oneness of God is not the end-all of belief, but all other beliefs spring from this fountain-head of eternal truth. This also delivers a message of liberation from all other yokes and releases man from all obligations except such as is born out of his submission to God.

This article has been further elucidated from different angles, both in the Holy Quran and the traditions of the Holy Prophet[sa] of Islam. For instance, the declaration 'La houl wala quat illa Billah' (There is no all-encompassing power except Allah) opens up new windows for a deeper and wider understanding of Unity. It negates all fears other than the fear of God. The second part of the same brings to the focus of attention another very important aspect of Unity, i.e. that the power to achieve good is solely dependent on God and that He is Master of all sources of strength and energy. Hence while the first part relates to the negative aspects of power, the second part relates to the positive.

In application to human actions, intentions and motivations etc., these two forces are all-encompassing. Man's intentions and his subsequent actions are always guided and controlled either by fear or hope and there is no exception to this rule. Those who do good deeds do so out of fear and hope, and those who indulge in vices are motivated by the same. The fears of non-believers belong to the negative ungodly category, and they shape their lives in accordance with these worldly fears. Sometimes they are afraid of earning the displeasure of monarchs and authorities, sometimes they are afraid of society in general or of despots and bullies. Again, sometimes they act evilly out of a fear of poverty and loss etc. So, in a world full of vices, a large part of human actions can be explained with reference to these fears.

The belief in Unity dispels these fears altogether and brings to one's mind the importance of the fear of God, which means that one must not be afraid of the displeasure of the ungodly, but should always endeavour to avoid displeasing God and shape one's life according to that fear alone. In the positive sense, the same applies to all human motivations and consequent actions. Man always lives by some motive to please someone, himself being no exception. In fact, more often than not, he works to please himself even at the cost of those who are otherwise dear to him.

A more exaggerated form of this attitude renders man a worshipper of his own ego. To achieve his purpose, man has to please those on whom his pleasures depend. As such, again he has to constantly strive to win the favours of monarchs, authorities etc. What we are describing is the worst form of slavery. The hopes and fears of a slave are completely dependent on the whims, pleasures and displeasures of his master. But a godless man has not one master alone. Every other human being in relation to his personal interests can play as God to him. If you analyse the ultimate cause of social, moral or political evils, it is such human worship which destroys the peace of man's mind, and society as a whole begins to deteriorate endlessly.

From this point of view, when you cast another glance at the fundamental declaration, that 'there is no God but Allah, the One and Only', all these fears and hopes relating to objects other than God are dispelled, as if by the waving of a magic wand. In other words, by choosing one master alone you are liberated from slavery to all others. To be a slave of such others as are themselves slaves to numberless gods is a poor bargain indeed! But that is not all. The gods that such people worship are many a time products of their own imagination, which can do them neither good nor harm. Most men, on the other hand, worship nothing but mortals like themselves, their own egos being supreme among them all. Hence each of them bows to numberless egotistic gods, their interests being at clash with each other, creating a situation which is the ultimate of chaos.

The Islamic concept of Unity also inculcates in man the realisation of the oneness of the human species, and does away with all such barriers as divide man into racial, ethnic and colour denominations. This gives birth to the universal concept of equality in Islam, which is its distinctive feature. Hence from the vantage point of God, all human beings, wherever and in whichever age they were born, stand equal in His sight. As will be demonstrated shortly, it is this fundamental which gives rise to all other fundamental beliefs and doctrines in Islam. As briefly mentioned before, Islam's doctrine of Unity is absolute and unsplittable; it has no room for adding to the Godhead in any form. He has neither a father nor a mother, nor has He a spouse. For Him to give birth to sons and daughters is inconceivable.

Another important aspect of Unity of God as presented by the Quran relates to absolute harmony in His creation. It is this harmony concept which appealed so strongly to Einstein. He was compelled to pay tribute to the perfect symmetry in nature, which according to him required the oneness of creator. He was a scientist, and his perception of that harmony was limited to the material universe. But the Holy Quran speaks of the harmony in creation in all its possible applications. The Holy Quran claims that within nature, as created by God, and within the divine books revealed by God, there is no disharmony; that there is complete concurrence between one area of God's creation and another, and between one book and the other.

It goes further to declare that there is perfect consistency between the Word of God and the Act of God and that there can be no contradiction between nature and the divine word as revealed to His prophets. This subject is beautifully expressed in the first five verses of *Surah Al-Mulk,* and is also taken up in many other verses of the Quran from various angles.

Coming to individuals, the belief in Unity plays a very important role in the education and upbringing of humans. It requires a consistency between man's views and actions, a consistency between his relationship with God and his fellow beings, thus binding creation in a single chain of unbreakable unity. This can be better understood by bringing to focus the practices of some so-called religious people, who preach hatred for one section of human society against another in the name of the one and only God. The principle of Unity of God is at variance with this practice and as such does not permit people to create divisions between God and His creation and within the creation of God.

Angels

The existence of angels is a universally accepted doctrine in different countries and different religions. However, they are sometimes discussed under other titles, the distinction being only one of nomenclature. Similarly, the nature of angels is understood differently among the followers of different religions.

Islam speaks of angels as celestial beings of a spiritual nature who have their own entity as persons. The major role they play is the transmission of messages from God to human beings. But they are misunderstood by many, even within Islam, as having human shape or some shape and form, which in fact is an inseparable idea from that of material existence. Matter must have shape and a well defined boundary. But spirit lies beyond the five dimensions of man's understanding. One can only believe in the existence of spirit if he is a religious person; otherwise it is beyond his reach to conceive the shape and form of spirits. Perhaps to resolve this problem and to make it easier for man to visualise angels, they are sometimes mentioned in religious books as appearing to holy people in the form of human beings. Not only that; they are also known to have appeared to some messengers of God in the form of certain birds. The Holy Ghost appeared to Jesus in the form of a dove:

> As soon as Jesus was baptised, he went up out of the water. At that moment heaven opened, and he saw the Spirit of God descending like a dove and lighting on him. (Matthew 3:16)

These various references found in religious books were perhaps largely responsible for the misperceptions about the form and nature of angels prevailing among the adherents of various religions. Out of angels, in some religions, *deyotas* and *gods* were created, while the original books may have only mentioned them as agencies specifically created by God for performing certain tasks in the universe; of this we have ample evidence in many divine books. So, it is not unlikely that some people misunderstand the significance of these statements and start treating angels as junior partners of God.

Let us now try to comprehend the nature of angels with reference only to the Quran and the traditions of the Holy Prophet[sa] of Islam, and not with reference to commonly held views. According to the Quran, the entire material universe as well as the entire religious universe is governed by certain spiritual powers, which are referred to as angels. Although some angels are referred to as single person, such as Gabriel, Michael or Israel, they in fact do not work alone. For each function there is one leader or one supreme angel who governs that function and under him works a host of angels, who are referred to in the Holy Quran as the *Junood of the Lord*. Whatever they do is completely subject to the will of God and the design that He has created for things. They cannot make the slightest deviation from the set course of functions allocated to them, or from the overall plan of things made by God.

According to the Quran, for each human being two angels are appointed to record good deeds and misdeeds, as the case may be. In this way the task of the angels is to organise the most intricate and profound system of recording. It does not mean that each has a book in his hand, jotting down in it whatever he observes. In fact, angels are responsible for a very complex system of registering the effect of man's deeds on his soul and personality so that a good man develops a healthy soul and a bad man breeds an unhealthy one.

The soul, as it is takes shape in every man till his death, needs a conscious organiser who transfers the effects of human thoughts, actions etc. to the soul. This is an intricate process not fully comprehended by man. However, we do partially witness this in the case of criminals acquiring a different visage from people of noble conduct. It is not at all impossible for anyone to observe such a difference, although it cannot be described in terms of black and white or other material terms. In fact the administration of the huge universe, right from its inception through the entire course of the billions of years of its evolutionary history, requires an enormous organisation of constant attention and control. This is performed by innumerable angels, who literally govern the vast universe and its intricate system of laws, as agents of God.

As far as the traditions go, we can comprehend to a degree the versatility of angels in being able to materialise in various forms or apparitions, which have no relation to their real form of existence which is beyond man's comprehension and has different dimensions from those known to us.

Once it is reported that a stranger suddenly entered the mosque where the Founder of Islam was sitting along with his companions. This man approached the assembly, sat respectfully in the front row and started to ask questions regarding the nature of Islam. Having finished his list of questions, he took leave and departed. Those present were amazed because first this man was a complete stranger who must have travelled some distance to reach the mosque. In small townships the knowledge of such visits does not remain a secret and everybody seems to know who has arrived and for what purpose. In his case, the arrival was so sudden that it appeared mysterious. Secondly, there were no marks of a journey on his bearing or his clothes. A fresh looking gentleman, he was of immaculately clean dress. Moreover the manner in which he began to ask questions without any introduction, and his abrupt departure, was extremely unusual to say the least.

Before the companions of the Holy Prophet[sa] could say anything, the Holy Prophet[sa] himself informed them that the person had actually been the angel Gabriel, who had asked the leading questions so that the companions could become acquainted with the facts contained in the answers given. Some companions ran out of the mosque to meet the angel in disguise, as they thought, but there was no trace of him anywhere. No-one in the township admitted to seeing such a man. As this incident is reported in the highly authentic books of tradition, we can safely infer that angels sometimes appear in ordinary human form for the purpose of discharging sundry errands. We find mention of angels in many other traditions, particularly in relation to the battles of Badr and Uhad, but it would be inappropriate perhaps to enter into a lengthy discourse on this issue.

As against the Quranic view explained above, almost in every country the commonly held view about angels among followers of various religions is more on the pattern of fairy tales than of them belonging to a celestial form of existence. They are said to have wings like birds or fairies, flapping them about as they fly from place to place. This misconception is perhaps born out of over-much literalising of religious terminology, which is cryptic and has, most often, metaphorical allusions. Thus we also find mention in the Holy Quran of wings in relation to angels, which speaks of them as having wings in twos, threes and fours:

الْحَمْدُ لِلّٰهِ فَاطِرِ السَّمَاوَاتِ وَالْأَرْضِ جَاعِلِ الْمَلَائِكَةِ رُسُلًا أُولِي أَجْنِحَةٍ مَثْنَى وَثُلَاثَ وَرُبَاعَ

All praise belongs to Allah the Maker of the heavens and the earth, Who employs the angels as messengers, having wings, two, three and four. (Quran 35: 2)

The Holy Quran has a very special style of elucidating all such passages where there lies a danger of obscurity. It does this with the help of other similar usages. The wings, for instance, are also mentioned in relation to a son's attitude towards his elderly parents. Building this subject, the Holy Quran admonishes the son to lower his wing of mercy over his parents, as they brought him up from the time of his infancy. *Wing* only means attributes and powers and we believe it is in this sense that wings are attributed to angels, or to persons claiming divine manifestation from among the various religions. For instance, in Gita, Krishna is known to have possessed four arms instead of two. There the extra pair of arms serves the same purpose as the wings found in other divine books.

Angels are responsible for controlling and maintaining the laws of nature. Virus and bacteria are governed, organised and maintained by specific angels, who work in harmony with each other to maintain a perfect balance. Similarly, eco-systems are not accidental or chaotic, but are regulated by the invisible, spiritual beings that we call angels.

THE CASE OF THE FALLEN ANGEL

There is another very much misunderstood episode concerning Satan. It is said, and it is believed, that prior to his fall he belonged to the category of angels. The Holy Quran rejects this view and presents Satan as possessing a fiery nature, thus belonging to such forms of life as are created from fire, for example the Jinn.

The Books

Let us now turn to the third article of faith, which is the belief in the books. Muslims are required to believe not only in the divine scripture revealed to the Holy Founder of Islam, which is called the Quran, but it is essential for every Muslim to believe in all such divine revelations as were vouchsafed to other prophets, from wherever and whichever age. It is an essential part of a Muslim's belief that if anyone professes belief only in the divine origin of the Quran and refuses to acknowledge the divine origin of other books, such as the Old Testament and the New Testament etc., his profession of Islam would be invalidated.

This belief resolves some problems but creates others, and needs to be studied at greater length. It provides the only foundation upon which the unity of man can be built on earth, in accordance with his belief in the Unity of God. It removes the root cause responsible for inter-religious disharmony and mistrust. But this belief in the divine origin of all books raises some very difficult questions to answer.

As we study the books that claim to be of divine origin, we find contradictions not only in the peripheral areas of their teachings, but also in the areas of basic and fundamental beliefs. This could not be so had they originated from the same eternal source of light. The case in point can well be illustrated by the fact that many such books contain passages which are understood and interpreted by their followers to lead to the belief in lesser deities sharing divinity with the one Supreme Being. In some books, God is presented as the head of a family of gods, having spouses, sons and daughters. In some other books, saintly human figures are attributed with such superhuman powers as are only befitting to be possessed by God. There are other books in which the Unity of God is stressed so strongly and uncompromisingly as to leave no room for anyone to share God's attributes in whatsoever capacity. The Quran stands out in this respect among all the scriptures of the major world religions.

How does the Quran resolve this dilemma? That is the question. According to the Quran, it is a universal trend of man to gradually interpolate the divine teachings which were vouchsafed to the founders of their religion. To change the concept of Unity to that of polytheism is a manifestation of the same trend. We can definitely discover evidence of the truth of this claim by tracing the history of changes in the text, or the interpretation of the text, from the time of its first revelation. This is why the Holy Quran pointedly draws our attention to the fact that all divine books concurred in their fundamental teachings only at the time of their inception. It is not necessary to go through the laborious exercise of pursuing the history of change, because logically there can be no other conclusion than the one made by the Quran. If there is no God other than the one Supreme Being, and if the claims of all religions that their divine books originated from God are to be accepted, then there has to be unanimity among all such books, at least in the fundamentals.

Having said that, one faces another important question regarding the manner in which one can ascertain the original doctrinal teachings common to all religions. One must find a logically acceptable methodology to sift the right from the wrong. The fundamental beliefs from the point of view of the Holy Quran are so attuned to human nature that they simply sink into the human hearts by the sheer force of their truth. They are as follows:

وَمَا أُمِرُوا إِلَّا لِيَعْبُدُوا اللَّهَ مُخْلِصِينَ لَهُ الدِّينَ حُنَفَاءَ وَيُقِيمُوا الصَّلَاةَ وَيُؤْتُوا الزَّكَاةَ وَذَلِكَ دِينُ الْقَيِّمَةِ

And they were not commanded but to serve Allah, being sincere to Him in obedience, and being upright, and to observe prayer, and pay

the Zakat. And that is the religion of the people of the right path.
(Quran 98:6)

This means that all the founders of the religions of the world were categorically told that they must worship the one and only God with all sincerity, dedicating them purely and completely to Him alone. They were also told to perform regular prayers (as institutionalised in their religion), and to spend (in the cause of God) for the needy and the destitute, and for other similar philanthropic purposes. It is hard to find disagreement with this, whichever religion one may belong to.

In this preliminary discourse we do not wish to involve ourselves in a lengthy discussion on the various different modes of worship as prescribed by God and the reasons for their being different. Presently we are focusing our attention on the reasons as to why religions appear to be different both in fundamentals and in the detailed teachings.

In short we can say that the hand of time is relentless, and the concept of decay is inseparable from the concept of time. Everything new must begin to grow old and change. One may look at the ruins of great castles and palaces with wonder, but even the buildings built by the same monarchs and designed by the same architects are no exception to this law. Sometimes they are added upon by later generations and are changed in design so drastically as to lose all resemblance to their original shape. Sometimes they are abandoned and become ruins. According to the Quran, the areas of uncompromisable differences in all religions are the handiworks of men belonging to later ages. In the light of this universally acceptable teaching of the Holy Quran, Islam seems to have paved the way for the unification of all religions, at least in fundamental principles. Thus it does away with man-made obstacles and barriers created to keep the religions apart as distinctly separate entities.

The reason mentioned above is not the only one responsible for the divergence in teachings observed in various books. Some differences were certainly not man-made, but were required by the dictates of time. As man gradually advanced in various areas of civilisation and culture, science and economy, at different stages of his history he required specific teachings related to that period of time, and a divine book would be revealed for his instruction. These time-related teachings were not universal, but related to specific situations and requirements. In certain ages, man lived a life not very far away from that of the sub-human species of life. His intellectual advancements were limited, his knowledge of the universe narrow. He was not even fully aware of the world that he inhabited. The modes of communication at his disposal were totally inadequate to help him understand the nature and vastness of the earth and the universality of man. Very often his awareness of existence was confined only to small areas of land or the country to which he belonged.

In many divine books revealed in those times, we do not find mention of the existence of the world beyond the limited domain of the people to whom the books were addressed. It does not necessarily mean, as some secular philosophers would have us believe, that this fact offers enough proof that the books in question were man-made rather than of divine origin.

All divine teachings were related to not only the requirements but also the information possessed by the people of the age, otherwise people of the age could have raised objections against the messengers of the time, accusing them of contradicting commonly established facts. This could have presented an insoluble dilemma for the prophets, as they themselves shared the same knowledge as the people. Many interesting examples of the same can be quoted from the Quran, where the understanding of nature as known to the people of the time was to be proved false by the men of learning of later ages. Whichever position the Quran adopted, it would still remain vulnerable to objections, either by contemporary people or by people of a later age. It is amazing how the Quran solves this problem, and in no way can it be criticised by present day philosophers and scientists either.

The following illustration would be of particular interest. A man of this age does not need to be highly educated to know that the earth rotates on its own axis; but if someone had made this statement fourteen hundred years ago and dared to attribute it to God, either he would have been rejected out of hand as being absolutely ignorant, or God would be ridiculed as having no knowledge of things which He professes to have created. The Holy Quran being a universal book for all ages could not have avoided the mention of this subject altogether, or the people of later ages, such as ours, would have rightfully blamed it for possessing no knowledge of the universe. Meeting this challenge squarely, the Holy Quran speaks of the mountains in the following verse, presenting them as floating or coasting like clouds, while people perceive them to be stationary:

وَتَرَى الْجِبَالَ تَحْسَبُهَا جَامِدَةً وَّهِيَ تَمُرُّ مَرَّ السَّحَابِ

You see the mountains and imagine them to be stationary whereas they are moving like the moving of clouds. (Quran 27:89)

Obviously the mountains would not be floating without the earth moving along with them. But the tense used is that of future (*Muzaria*) which is common to both the continuous present and future. So the verse may be translated as: 'The mountains are moving constantly in a coasting motion without making the least effort on their part.' It can also be translated as, 'The mountains will move as if they were sailing.' People of that age might have taken refuge in this second option, but they forgot to take notice of another part of the same verse which says, 'While you think they are stationary.' How could the man of any age think the mountains to be stationary if they suddenly started moving? The description of their movement leaves no room anywhere for anyone to be alive on earth and watch quietly the amazing phenomenon mentioned in the verse.

Logically therefore, the only valid translation would be: 'While you consider the mountains to be stationary, in fact they are constantly in motion.' There are many other similar examples which can be quoted from the Quran, but I have already illustrated them in another address of mine entitled *Rationality and Revelation in Relation to Knowledge and Truth*. Any reader interested in further study could refer to the same.

We know for certain that during the remote past when the Vedas were revealed for the benefit of the people of India, the Indians had little knowledge of the worlds lying beyond the seas. Hence there is no mention of any country or people outside India, across the natural boundaries of the Himalayas on the one side and the seas on the other. The silence of the Vedas on the subject may be an appropriate and well understood silence on the part of God. It must be made clear that the facts mentioned in the divine books are of two categories. The first category comprises these worldly facts, which can be understood and verified by all human beings regardless of which religion they belong to. These are the facts that we are referring to in the above discussion. As far as facts belonging to the otherworldly things are concerned, any man can make any claim about them, because they lie beyond the human reach of verification.

Despite differences however, the fundamental points of similarities are always traceable if one digs deeply into a study of original books. As an archaeologist can reconstruct the design of the original plan from a study of the ruins, so also it should not be difficult for a keen observer to read the message of Unity even through the veils of fog and mist created by the followers of the religions as they move away from the time of the founding prophets.

We briefly mentioned some differences which were intentionally designed as against those which resulted from the interpolation of man. To illustrate the former, we can refer to a teaching of the Torah which seems to deprive the Jewish people of the option of forgiveness. To a casual observer, from the vantage point of the modern age, it would appear to be a rather ungodly teaching, unbalanced in the favour of vengeance. Yet a closer examination of the requirements of that age would present the teaching in a completely different light. We know that the Children of Israel, under the oppressive and despotic rules of Pharaohs, were deprived of all their fundamental human rights. They were forced to live a life of abasement and slavery, which did not recognise their right to defend themselves and hit back at the oppressor.

Some two centuries of such an abject way of life had virtually robbed them of their upright noble human qualities. They would much rather give up their right to avenge in the name of forgiveness, just another name for utter cowardice. Had they been given the clear option to either take revenge or forgive, few there would be among them who would dare take the former option. As such the teaching of the Torah, though seemingly harsh and over-much one sided, is the most perfect teaching in relation to the requirements of that time. It was a diseased state which was meant to be cured with the bitter pill of this injunction.

About thirteen centuries of practising merciless vengeance had indeed hardened the hearts of the Israelites into those of stone. It was at this juncture of time that the Messiah came, who was himself forgiveness, love and modesty personified. Had God granted the Jews of his time both the options of forgiveness and revenge, they would certainly have opted for revenge without even dreaming of forgiveness. The question arises as to what should be the perfect teaching relevant to the time of Jesus? Forgiveness of course, but without the option of revenge. This is exactly what happened. This illustration makes it amply clear that certain teachings, though apparently contradictory, in fact serve the same purpose and work in unison as far as the designs of God are concerned. The purpose is the healing of the sick which may need different medicines at different times.

The Prophets

The fourth fundamental article of faith in Islam is belief in all the prophets. This article is in fact a logical conclusion to the third one. The same philosophy as underlies the belief in all books also neccssitates belief in all the prophets. The Holy Quran speaks of the many prophets who mostly belong to the Middle Eastern line of prophethood, beginning with Adam[as] up to the time of Muhammad, peace be upon him. But there are exceptions to the rule. There are two things which are specifically mentioned in the Quran relating to this issue:

* ❖ Although the names and short histories of some prophets were revealed to the Holy Founder of Islam, the list is in no way exhaustive. They are just specimen names and there are a large number of prophets who do not find mention in the Quran.
* ❖ In the list of prophets who are specifically mentioned, there are certain names which do not seem to belong to the prophets of Israel. Many commentators therefore are inclined to believe that they are non-Arab prophets who are included in the list just for the sake of representation of the outer world. For instance, Dhul-Kifl is one name in the list of prophets which is unheard of in the Arab or Semitic references. Some scholars seem to have traced this name to Buddha, who was of Kapeel, which was the capital of a small state situated on the border of India and Nepal. Buddha not only belonged to Kapeel, but was many a time referred to as being 'Of Kapeel'. This is exactly what is meant by the word 'Dhul-Kifl'. It should be remembered that the consonant 'p' is not present in Arabic and the nearest one to it is 'fa'. Hence, Kapeel transliterated into Arabic becomes *Kifl*.

Apart from the evidence of the Quran, there is one reference which is controversial among the commentators. There is a tradition reported from the Holy Prophet[sa] which speaks of an Indian prophet by name. In his words:

كان فى الهند نبيا اسود اللون اسمه كاهنا

There was a prophet of God in India who was dark in colour and his name was 'Kahan'.

Now anyone acquainted with the history of Indian religions would immediately connect this description to Lord Krishna, who is invariably described in the Hindu literature as being dark of complexion. Also, the title *Kanhaya* is added to his name *Krishna*. *Kanhaya* contains the same consonants *K, N, H* as does the name *Kahan*—in no way an insignificant similarity. But whether any non-Arab prophet was mentioned by name or not is only an academic discussion. There is no denying the fact that the Holy Quran makes it incumbent on every Muslim not only to believe in all the prophets, but it also clearly informs us that in every region of the world and in every age, God did raise messengers and prophets.

This belief in principle in the truth of the founding prophets and also the minor prophets of other religions is a unique declaration of the Quran, absent in all other divine books. It throws light on the universality of creation as well as on the universality of Islam itself. If the Quranic claim that the teachings of the Quran are for the entire world is true, then it has to recognise the truth of all prophets. Otherwise the followers of so many different religions will not find any connecting bridge between themselves and Islam.

The recognition of the truth of all books and the recognition of the truth of all prophets is a revolutionary declaration which has many benefits for man as a whole. Among other things, it powerfully paves the way for inter-religious peace and harmony. How can one be at peace with the followers of other religions if one considers them to be impostors and if one monopolises the truth only for the religious divines of one's own faith?

It is a universal observation that the followers of various religions tend to know very little about the doctrinal aspects of their own religions. It is the ordained priesthood or other leaders who seem to be the custodians of religious knowledge, and it is to them that the common people turn when they stand in need of religious guidance. Such people are far more sensitive to the question of the honour of their prophets and divines than they are even on the issue of God and His honour.

Apart from Islam, none of the divine books of religions bear testimony to the truth of the founders of other religions. The absence of any recognition of the truth of prophets other than their own has insulated religions from one another, each one claiming to monopolise truth, each viewing the prophets of other religions as impostors. Although in every day life we do not find this expressed in such strong terms, the hard reality remains that if the followers of any religion take their beliefs seriously they have to consider all other religions to be false, even at their sources. It is impossible to conceive a Christian, a true believer in Christianity as he understands it today, who would testify to the truth of Buddha, Krishna and Zoroaster. Particularly, the Christians' stance against the Holy Prophet[sa] of Islam is exactly the one mentioned above; they have to denounce him as an impostor, otherwise the only alternative for them is to become Muslims. The Orientalists discussing this subject have always maintained this position very clearly, many among them having gone to the extent of showing undisguised hostility towards the Founder of Islam on the premise that he had to be false. The same applies to other religions alike.

Although in every day life we do not come across such glaring examples of discourtesy and insult, but whether one keeps one's views to oneself or expresses them openly, the barrier still remains. It is evident from this that the followers of all religions have compartmentalised themselves against all others, and the barrier between truth and falsehood, right or wrong does succeed in preventing the religious harmony so much needed by man today.

Of course, there are very civilised and educated Christians in the world, who out of courtesy would not offend the sensibilities of Muslims by denouncing the Holy Prophet[sa] of Islam as an impostor. However the Christians, in accordance with their beliefs, have no option but to reject the truth of the Founder of Islam. In the case of a Muslim however, it is a completely different story. When he speaks of Jesus Christ[as] or Moses[as] or Krishna or Buddha with veneration and love, he does so because he has no other option. It is a part of the fundamental article of his faith to extend not just a human courtesy, but to genuinely believe in their truth and honour. In the light of this, this article of faith appears to hold an importance of global scale. It establishes inter-religious peace and harmony and genuinely creates an atmosphere of mutual trust and love. Like the Unity of God it holds the intrinsic quality of being irreplaceable—there is no alternative.

The Promised Messiah, Hadhrat Mirza Ghulam Ahmad[as] of Qadian, has summarised the Islamic belief in other prophets as follows:

One of the principles which forms the basis of my belief refers to the established religions of the world. These religions have met with wide acceptance in various regions of the earth. They have acquired a measure of age, and have reached a stage of maturity. God has informed me that none of these religions were false at their source and none of the prophets impostors.[3]

This is a beautiful principle, which promotes peace and harmony, and which lays the foundation for reconciliation, and which helps the moral condition of man. All prophets that have appeared in the world, regardless of whether they dwelt in India or Persia or China, or in some other country, we believe in the truth of them, one and all.[4]

With the establishment of this fact that there had to be prophets all over the world in all ages who originated from God, the stage seems to be set for a universal prophet. The acceptance of a universal prophet requires a reciprocity. When you expect others to believe in someone you consider to be true, it would certainly help if you bear witness to the truth of such holy people in whom the other party has unshakeable faith.

Islam therefore lays down the foundation for the universality of a single prophet. As such the claim of the Quran that the Holy Prophet[sa] was raised not only for Arabia but for the whole of mankind, is founded on a sound philosophy. We find mention in every religion of a utopian future or golden age when all mankind would be brought under the one flag. But there does not seem to be any foundation laid for the unification of man in his beliefs and dogmas. It was for the first time in the history of religion that Islam paved the way for a universal

---

3   Translated from the original Urdu *Tohfa Qaisariya* p. 256, *Roohani Khazain* (Spiritual Treasures), Vol 12, Unwin Brothers, Gresham Press, Old Woking, Surrey, 1984.

4   *ibid.* p. 259

religion by the declaration that all the people of the world, at different times, were blessed with the advent of divine messengers.

According to the Holy Quran, the institution of prophethood is universal and timeless. There are two terms used to indicate the same office, each with slightly different connotations. The term *An-Nabi* has the connotation of prophecy. Those whom God chooses to represent Him are implanted with the knowledge of certain important events regarding the future. They are also told of things past which were unknown to the people, and his knowledge of them stands as a sign of his being informed by an All-Knowing Being. The prophecy as such establishes the truth of the prophets so that people may submit to them and accept their message.

The second term used in connection with prophets, is *Al-Rasool* or Messenger. This refers to such contents of the prophet's revelation as deal with important messages to be delivered to mankind on God's behalf. Those messages could be speaking of a new code of law, or they could simply be admonishing people for their past lapses in reference to previous revealed laws. Both these functions unite in a single person, and as such all prophets can be termed as messengers and all messengers as prophets.

According to Islam, all prophets are human beings and none bear superhuman characteristics. Wherever some miracles are attributed to prophets, who are understood to indicate their superhuman character, the categorical and clear statements of the Quran reject such a notion. Raising of the dead is one of such miracles attributed to certain prophets. Although similar descriptions are found in many divine scriptures or religious books, according to the Quran they are not meant to be taken literally, but have a metaphorical connotation. For instance, it is attributed to Jesus[as] that he raised the dead into a new life. But the Holy Quran speaks of the Holy Prophet Muhammad[sa] in the same terms, with the same words being applied to his miracle of spiritual revival. Similar is the case of creating birds out of clay and causing them to fly in the name of God. These birds are only human beings who are bestowed with the faculty of spiritual flight, as against the earthly people.

No prophet is granted an exceptionally long term of life which makes him distinctly different and above the brotherhood of prophets to which he belongs. Nor is any prophet mentioned as having risen bodily to remote recesses of the universe. Wherever there is such mention, it is spiritual ascent which is meant, not bodily ascent, which the Quran categorically declares is against the character of prophets. When the Holy Founder of Islam was required by the People of the Book to physically ascend to heaven and bring back a book, the answer which God taught him was simply this:

$$قُلۡ سُبۡحَانَ رَبِّیۡ هَلۡ كُنۡتُ إِلَّا بَشَرًا رَّسُوۡلًا$$

Say to them: 'My Lord is far above (such childish conduct). I am no more than a human being and a prophet.' (Quran 17:94)

This answer rejects all claims about other prophets who are understood to have ascended physically to heaven. The argument implied in this answer is that no human being and no prophet can rise bodily to heaven, otherwise the Prophet Muhammad[sa] could also have repeated the same miracle. The emphasis on the human characteristics of prophets and their human limitations is one of the most beautiful features of fundamental Islamic teachings. Prophets rise above their fellow human beings not because they were gifted with superhuman qualities, but only because they gave a better

account of the qualities that they had been gifted with. They
remained human despite having ascended to great spiritual heights,
and their conduct as such is inimitable by other human beings.

On the issue of continuity of prophecy, Islam categorically
declares the Holy Prophet[sa] of Islam to be the last of the law-bearing
prophets and the Quran to be the last divine book of law, perfected
and protected till the end of time. Obviously a book which is perfect
and also protected from interpolation transcends alteration. No
change is warranted on both counts. As long as a book is perfect and
protected from human interpolation, no change is justified.

As far as prophecy other than law-bearing prophecy is concerned,
the possibility of its continuity is clearly mentioned in the Quran.
Again there are clear prophecies about such divine reformers as
would be completely subordinate to the Holy Founder of Islam and
the Holy Book—the Quran. The following verse of Surah Al-Nisa leaves
no ambiguity about this:

وَمَن يُطِعِ اللَّهَ وَالرَّسُولَ فَأُولَٰئِكَ مَعَ الَّذِينَ أَنْعَمَ اللَّهُ عَلَيْهِم مِّنَ النَّبِيِّينَ وَالصِّدِّيقِينَ
وَالشُّهَدَاءِ وَالصَّالِحِينَ وَحَسُنَ أُولَٰئِكَ رَفِيقًا

*And whoso obeys Allah and this Messenger of His shall be among
those on whom Allah has bestowed His blessings, namely, the
Prophets, the Truthful, the Martyrs, and the Righteous. (Quran 4:70)*

In short, Islam is declared in the Quran to be the last perfected
religion for the benefit of mankind, after which no new teaching
would be revealed to annul the teachings of Islam, nor would a new
independent prophet be born outside the domain of Islam; any new
prophet would be completely subordinate to the Holy Prophet
Muhammad[sa].

The prophets always came to deliver a message. That message was not confined to the areas of beliefs, but also covered the areas of practices and implementation of the beliefs. The teachings are divided into two large categories:

* How to improve one's relationship with God.
* How to conduct oneself in relation to one's fellow human beings.

These two categories in fact cover all aspects of religious laws. We cannot enter into a lengthy discussion of how this task is carried out to perfection in Islam, but perhaps it would be appropriate to illustrate a few important features of this teaching of universal character.

Prayer

Worship is common to all religions. What differs is only the manner and style of worship. That which is unique in Islamic mode of worship is that it contains features from the mode of prayers found in other religions. Some people pray to God in a standing posture and some in a sitting posture. In some religions people remember God by kneeling to Him, while others bow down to Him. Some stand before Him with folded arms and others with arms hanging at their sides. In short there is no single mode of worship common to all religions as a whole. It is fascinating however to note that Islam instructs its followers concerning the manner of prayer so comprehensively that all the postures of worship found in other religions are symbolically represented in the Muslim prayer. Another step forward in the direction of ushering in an era of universal religion, it seems.

The institution of Islamic prayer is a most highly developed system, covering every human requirement. It should be remembered at the outset that the purpose of worship is not just bowing to a Superior Being and paying homage to His greatness, as if God created man only for satiating His egotistic desire of being praised. All the purposes mentioned in relation to the philosophy of worship and the manner in which a Muslim is required to conduct his prayer, makes it manifestly clear that the benefit of prayer is drawn by the worshipper himself and in no way can it be taken as a favour to God. The Holy Quran declares that God does not stand in need of men's praises. He is so great in His nobility and so sublime in His character that the praises of His creatures do not add anything to His magnanimity and majesty. The Holy Prophet[sa] of Islam once mentioned that if the entire mankind had turned away from God and committed the worst possible sins, one and all, they would not diminish His universal grandeur even as much as when someone dips a sharp needle into a vast ocean; the water one finds adhered to the surface of the needle would be far more than the sins of the entire mankind could take away from the glory of God.

So, worship in the Holy Quran is only prescribed for the sake of the worshipper himself. It is a vast subject and we can only illustrate a few points in relation to this as mentioned in the Holy Quran and the traditions of the Holy Prophet of Islam.

Remembrance of God and pondering over His attributes during the prayer helps man in refining his spirit, bringing it more into harmony with the nature of God. This is central to the Islamic prayer. Man was made in the image of his creator and he must ever strive to gain

closeness to Him. This is a lesson in nobility which is ultimate. Those
who train themselves to think like God and to act like Him within the
limitations of the human sphere, constantly improve in their relation
to all other human beings and even other forms of life.

In human terms it can be better understood with respect to a
mother's attitude towards her children. For the one who truly gains
nearness to a mother, all that is dear to the mother will naturally
become dear to him as well. Acquiring the attitude of the creator is
like acquiring the attitude of an artist to his works of art. It is
impossible for one to be near God and distance himself from His
creation. Again, the term used for worship in the Quran is derived
from a word which is so significant and different from terms used in
other religions. *Ain, Be, Dael* ('A', 'B', 'D') are the three root letters
which have the basic meaning of slavery. Like a slave who loses
everything to his master and follows him in all respects, the
worshipper in Islam must do the same in his relation to God. The
infinitive used for worship has the connotation of following in the
footsteps of someone. That is the ultimate in the imitation of God's
attributes. The Quran also says:

$$ إِنَّ الصَّلَاةَ تَنْهَى عَنِ الْفَحْشَاءِ وَالْمُنْكَرِ $$

*Verily, Prayer prevents the worshipper from indulging in anything
that is undignified or indecent. (Quran 29:46)*

This verse has both positive and negative connotations, both highly
essential for cultivating ideal human conduct. Thus in its negative
connotation, it helps the worshipper by liberating him from sins of all
types. In its positive connotation it educates man, refines his

character and cultivates his qualities to such sublimity as to make him worthy of communion with God.

Another area which is highly important in this regard is the role that worship plays in developing one's soul. According to Islam, each human soul in relation to the carnal human body can be likened unto a child in the uterus of the mother. To give birth to a healthy child requires so many influences that are constantly transferred from the mother to the embryo and the child at a later stage. If the mother's influences on the embryo are unhealthy, the child is born as congenitally ill; if they are healthy then the child is born enjoying perfect health. Of all the influences that work towards the making and modification of the human soul, prayer is the most important single factor.

The institution of Islamic prayer is rich in so many profound lessons as are not found even fractionally in other religions. Islam admonishes both congregational and individual prayer. The congregational prayers are held in a manner which is amazingly well organised and meaningful.

There is one leader who leads the congregation in all such prayers. That leader is not an ordained priest; anyone whom the people consider worthy of this task is chosen as the *Imam*. The assembly is admonished to be arrayed behind the Imam in perfectly straight lines, each worshipper standing close to the other, shoulder to shoulder, with no distance between any two worshippers. They follow the Imam perfectly in everything that he does. As he bows they bow, as he stands they stand. As he prostrates they prostrate. Even if the Imam commits a mistake and does not condone it even after a reminder, all followers must repeat the same. To question the Imam during the prayer is not permitted. All face the same direction without exception, facing the first house of worship ever built for the benefit of mankind. No-one is permitted to reserve any special place behind the Imam. In this regard the rich and poor are treated with absolute equality, so also the old and the young. Whoever reaches the mosque ahead of others has the prior option to sit wherever he pleases. None has the right to remove others from the place that they occupy, except for reasons of security etc., in which case it becomes an administrative measure. Thus the Islamic system of prayer is rich not only in spiritual instruction but also in communal and organisational instruction.

All mosques are frequented five times a day, a task which appears to be over-much demanding to a casual observer. This aspect should be further elaborated to build a more comprehensive picture of the role of congregational prayers in the Muslims' way of life. Of course in an ideal Muslim society, where mosques are provided within reach of almost every citizen, the five time congregational prayer becomes a routine way of all Muslims' life. The Midday Prayer, which ordinarily is more problematic, is performed in Muslim societies during the midday break from work. Thus it is not only a lunch break, but is slightly extended to accommodate the performance of prayer as well. The next prayer after the midday prayer is the Afternoon Prayer, which is performed almost immediately after return from an ordinary day's work. Then no prayer is permitted until after sunset. The time between the two is spent in outdoor activities like sports, shopping, walks, visits to friends and relatives etc. It is a period of relaxation in which prayers are practically forbidden, except for the quiet remembrance of God which becomes a constant feature with some believers. At sunset, the night of the believer begins with the Sunset Prayer, after which there is again a time for relaxation, dining, and so on. The night is capped before retirement with the last prayer which is called *Isha*. It is discouraged to stay awake after Isha in wasteful occupations of gossip and vain talk etc.

The Muslims are encouraged to acquire a habit of early to bed and early to rise. The day, next morning, begins routinely in the small hours before dawn. The prayer which is performed at the end of the night is called *Tahajjud*. It is not obligatory, but is a very highly emphasised optional prayer. The dawn ushers in the time for Morning Prayer, which is called *Al-Fajar*. Optional prayers are not recommended between Fajar and sunrise, for obvious reasons. Then till *Zuhar*, the midday prayer, only two optional prayers are mentioned; otherwise the pre-*Zuhar* period is expected to be spent in normal day to day activities.

Looking at the institution of prayer in Islam from another angle, it is intriguing to note how well organised, disciplined and comprehensive it is. There are certain prayers of congregation in which recitation of the Quran is done in a loud, audible voice, in a semi-singing tone, which does not exactly conform to the concept of singing, but which has a rhythmical tone that is deeply penetrating. The Holy Prophet[sa] also advised that there should be a shadow of sadness in the tone in which the Quran is recited; this makes it more touching, with the meaning of the verses sinking deeper into the recesses of the heart. In some prayers, particularly the two afternoon prayers, there is no loud chanting; this goes well with the general mood of the time. Even the birds cease to sing during the early parts of the afternoon and there is a general air of silence covering the hubbub of normal work. The Morning Prayer, the prayer after sunset and the prayer after the fall of night all include periods where chanting of verses is the routine practice.

The prayer can be further divided into two categories. As against congregational prayers, individual prayers are also highly emphasised. In congregational prayers, society pays homage to God collectively and openly. In individual prayers, emphasis is laid on privacy and there should be no effort to display such prayers to anyone. Similarly the late night prayer is performed in perfect privacy. Members of the same house try to find their own niches and even husband and wife try to say their prayers separately, so that communion with God becomes a highly personal affair.

It has been observed that the institution of the five time congregational prayer has worked very well, for over fourteen hundred years or so, for the protection and preservation of this holy institution. The mosques have been the mainstay in keeping this noble institution alive. They also serve as education centres for young and old and throughout history they have played the most prominent role in religious teachings and instruction.

The places of worship in Islam, whether congregational or private, are kept meticulously clean. Everyone is expected to take his shoes off before entering such places. Although in every prayer the worshipper has to touch the floor with his forehead, sometimes briefly and sometimes for longer periods, it is surprising that no skin diseases have been transferred from forehead to forehead in the Muslim society. Some may attribute this to the high standard of cleanliness and some to the blessings of God, but this is a well observed fact.

As far as the contents of the prayer go, they are of two types:

1. A formal routine recitation of verses of the Quran and other prayers which are done essentially in the language of the Quran, which is Arabic. All worshippers are expected to know the

meaning of what they are reciting, otherwise they will deprive themselves of the immense benefit which they may draw from the meaningful recitation. It will make this discussion too lengthy if we were to go into the details of the contents, but such readers as are interested in further study can always consult the relevant literature.

2. To the second category belong the individual prayers in one's own language in which one is free to beg as he pleases. This second category is controversial in the sense that many a school of jurisprudence disallow such practices and insist on the recitation of only the prescribed form, irrespective of whether the worshipper understands that or not. However, they do appreciate the need for private and personal prayers, so they suggest praying in one's own language after the formal prayer has ended and not during its course. We, the Ahmadi Muslims, recommend and practice the former option of praying to God in one's own language as one pleases during the formal prayer.

As we have amply demonstrated above, the institution of Islamic prayer is a highly developed one, where the individual is required to pray five times a day, both individually and in congregation with others. Islamic prayer thus plays an important role in the life of a Muslim and in the spiritual and moral upbringing of the individual.

Spending in the Cause of Allah

Now turning to alms and other philanthropic spending, all religions seem to promote the same in one way or another. In some religions spending in the cause of Allah is institutionalised by levying a well defined tithe. In others, the method is left to the free will of the individual as to how and how much to spend. Again, in this area the universality of Islamic teachings becomes evident when a detailed study of this subject is made from the Quran and the tradition and practices of the Holy Prophet of Islam[sa]. The subject is so vast, that it covers all possible areas of human interest.

We find in Islam an institutionalised mode of spending as well as non-institutionalised modes of spending, with their respective spheres well defined. But Islam does not leave it at that. It speaks of all possible requirements and their relative importance. Islam goes further to instruct man to spend in the cause of Allah keeping in view all the "do's" and "don'ts" mentioned in the Quran. The Holy Quran is very clear on which spending in the cause of Allah will find favour with Him and which will be rejected. The subject is so vast, as mentioned before, that it is beyond the scope of this short treatise to cover every aspect of it. One thing however is certain, that the character of universality of this teaching becomes more and more apparent as one proceeds to grasp its form and spirit. Islam also clearly defines the areas of spending of the prescribed religious tithes, leaving no ambiguity whatsoever.

Hajj

Another example which demonstrates the universality of Islamic injunctions regarding the practice of religion is the instance of Hajj, the pilgrimage. Once again one finds the institution of pilgrimage in all religions of the world, but the sites for pilgrimage are scattered at different places in one or more countries. One does not find a single central place which all the followers of a religion must visit at least once in their lifetime. Amazingly in Islam we find exactly such a place in Mecca, where Muslims from all over the world are expected to gather and spend about ten days entirely dedicated to the memory of God. The pilgrims come from all countries, all nations, and all races and in all ages. Men, women and children, they all gather once a year for a fantastic rally which sometimes runs into the millions. This grand display of universality is seen nowhere else in any other religion. Hence all these fingers, which were raised in different areas of Islamic teaching, point to the same message of unification of man on earth under the Unity of God.

The institution of pilgrimage can be traced back to the time of Abraham[as], peace be upon him. But there are very clear statements in the Quran describing it as an ancient institution, starting from times immemorial when the first House of God was built in Mecca. In the olden times Mecca was pronounced *Baka*, so the Holy Quran refers to the first house as being built not in Mecca but in *Baka*. It is also called *Bait-ul-Ateeq*, or the most ancient house. Abraham[as] raised it from the ruins which he discovered under divine guidance, and about which he was commissioned by God to rebuild with the help of his son Ishmael[as]. It is the same place where he had left his wife Hagar and infant son Ishmael[as], again under divine instruction. But work on the House of God awaited attention until Ishmael[as] grew to an age where he could be of some help. So, both of them worked together to rebuild the house and restart the institution of pilgrimage.

Many rites performed during pilgrimage are rooted in those early days of the reconstruction of the House of God, and some even go beyond that. For instance, the running between Safa and Marwah, two small hillocks close to the House of God, is done in memory of Hagar's search for some sign of human presence to help her and her child in their dire hour of need. The child is described as having become extremely restive with the agony of thirst, striking the earth with his heels in desperation. There, it is said, sprouted a fountain which still exists today in some form. Later, a well which was created around that spot and its water is considered to be the blessed water. Most of the pilgrims who perform the Hajj try to bring some water from there by way of blessing for their relatives and friends.

There are other rites and traditions which should be briefly explained. In Hajj the pilgrims do not wear any sewn garments; rather, they dress in two loose sheets. This is further indicative of the tradition being most ancient. It indicates that the institution of Hajj began when man had not learnt to wear sewn clothes. They had only started to cover themselves. As such it seems that it is in memory of those ancient people who used to circuit the first house built for the worship of God in that preliminary dress that the pilgrims are required to do the same. Again, the shaving of the head is an important feature which is also universally found as a symbol of dedication among monks, priests, hermits and vishnus. This further adds to the universality of its character. Women are exempt from shaving, but they have to symbolically cut their hair as a token. Also, in the places where Hadrat Abraham[as] is known to have remembered God in the style of an intoxicated lover and extolled his glory with loud chanting, the pilgrims are required to do the same in the same places.

Fasting

Fasting is another form of worship found universally in the world religions. Although there are vast differences regarding the mode of fasting and the conditions applied to it, the central idea of fasting is present everywhere. Where it is not mentioned clearly, it is likely that it may have either been discontinued or have petered out through gradual decay in practice. The case of Buddha is an interesting example. He started his quest for truth with a severe form of fasting, but later on it is said that he abandoned this practice because it had adversely affected his health. In view of this one can understand why he discontinued, but this does not in any way indicate that he had ceased to believe in fasting. Perhaps that is why some Buddhists, here and there, still observe some form of fasting.

Fasting in Islam is a highly developed institution, and needs to be studied in depth. There are two types of injunctions with regards to fasting. One relates to obligatory fasting and the other to optional. Obligatory fasting is further divided into two categories:

1. There is one full month in every year in which fasting is prescribed for Muslims all over the world. As the month is a lunar month, so it keeps changing around the year in relation to the solar months. This creates a universal balance for the worshippers. Sometimes the fasting in winter months is easy as far as the days go, in comparison to the long winter nights, while during the summer months the days become long and exacting. As the lunar months keep rotating around the year, so Muslims in all parts of the world have some periods of easy fasting and some of arduous fasting.

Fasting in Islam begins everywhere at the first appearance of dawn and ends with sunset. During this period one is expected to abstain from all food and drink completely. It is not just physical hunger and thirst that constitute the Muslim fast, but the nights prior to the beginning of the fast acquire a far more important character and play a central role in the institution of fasting. The Muslims wake up many hours before dawn for individual prayer and the remembrance of God. Also the Holy Quran is recited in every Muslim house much more than in ordinary days. A greater part of the night is thus spent in spiritual exercises which make up the very essence of fasting.

During the day, apart from restraining from food and water, all Muslims are particularly exhorted to refrain from vain talk, quarrels and fights, or from any such occupation as is below the dignity of a true believer. No indulgence in carnal pleasure is allowed; even husband and wife during the day lead separate lives, except for the formal human relationship common to all people.

In Islam, alms-giving and care for the destitute is so highly emphasised that it becomes part of a Muslim's daily life. However when it comes to Ramadhan, the month of fasting, Muslims are required to redouble their efforts in this field. It is reported of the Holy Prophet[sa] that spending in the cause of the poor was a routine daily practice with him which has been likened unto a breeze, never ceasing to bring comfort and solace to the needy. However during Ramadhan, the reporters of the *Ahadith*, the sayings of the Holy Prophet[sa] remind us that the breeze seemed to pick up speed and blow like strong winds. Alms-giving and care for the destitute are so highly emphasised that in no period during the year do Muslims engage in such philanthropic purposes as they do during the month of Ramadhan.

2.   Other obligatory fasting is most often related to the condoning of sins by God. This also includes violation of the obligatory fasts.

The optional fasting is so well promoted that it becomes a part of the righteous Muslim's way of life. Although a majority of Muslims do not go beyond the month of obligatory fasting, some keep fasts now and then particularly when in trouble. As it is expected that the prayers offered in fasting are more productive, some people keep extra fasts to ward off their problems, but some do it only for the sake of winning Allah's special favours. There is no limit to this, except that the Founder of Islam strongly discouraged those who had vowed to fast continuously for their whole life. When the Holy Prophet[sa] came to learn of one such case, he disapproved of the practice and censured the man for attempting to achieve liberation as if by forcing his will upon God. He told the person concerned that, 'By putting yourself to trouble or discomfort, not only will you be unable to please God, but you may even earn His displeasure.' He pointed out that over emphasis on austerity is likely to make one negligent towards one's wife and children, kith and kin, friends etc.

The Holy Prophet[sa] reminded him specifically of his responsibilities in the area of human relationship; 'Do your duty to God as well as to the creation of God equitably' was the advice. To some, after their insistent petulant begging, he permitted optional fasts only in the style of David[as], peace be upon him. The Holy Founder of Islam told them that it was the practice of David to fast one day and abstain from doing so the next. Throughout his life, after he made this vow, he kept the fast on alternate days. So the Holy Prophet[sa] said, 'I can only permit you that much and no more.'

The institution of fasting is extremely important because it cultivates the believer in almost every area of his spiritual life. Among other things, he learns through personal experience about what hunger, poverty, loneliness and discomforts mean to the less fortunate sections of society. Abstention from even such practices during the month of Ramadhan as are permissible in everyday life plays a constructive role in refining the human character.

The Holy War

This is a very important issue which relates to the propagation of all divine messages. It relates to the instrument of propagation. Adherents of almost all religions, as they move away in time from the source, are invariably known to have employed coercion either to keep people within the fold of their religion, or to convert others into their faith. But according to the Holy Quran, this in no way reflects upon their religion's attitude to coercion. No religion at its source has ever permitted the use of force in any form whatsoever. In fact all religions have been made targets of coercion and no efforts were spared by their opponents to arrest the growth of religions at their source and to annihilate them completely. Every time a new prophet came, attempts were invariably made by the enemies to suppress his message through the use of force and merciless persecution. It is the most tragic irony therefore that of all the books, the Holy Quran is singled out today as proponent of the employment of coercion for the sake of the spread of its message. Even greater tragedy lies in the fact that it is the Muslim clergy itself which loudly propounds this view, blatantly attributing it to the Holy Quran.

The Holy Quran, it should be remembered, is the only divine book which absolves all the prophets of the world, wherever and in whichever age they were born, of the crime of coercion in relation to the spread of their message. Hence it is inconceivable that the Quran should present its Holy Prophet[sa] as the harbinger of an era of bloodshed in the name of peace and hatred in the name of love of God. This is no place to engage in intricate polemical discussions, so this brief introduction should suffice here. According to the Quran, the Holy War, called *Jihad*, is in reality a holy campaign which uses the help of the Quran to bring about a spiritual revolution in the world.

$$\text{وَجَاهِدْهُمْ بِهِ جِهَادًا كَبِيرًا}$$

Fight against them by means of it (the Quran) a great fight. (Quran 25:53)

These are the very words of the Quran which throw light on the nature of Jihad. It must be fought by means of the Quran and the Quranic message alone. Again, to tame one's rebellious nature into complete submission to God is another form of Jihad which is in fact the greater Jihad, according to the Holy Prophet[sa] of Islam. On returning from a battle, he is reported to have said:

$$\text{رجعنا من الجهاد الاصغر الى الجهاد الاكبر}$$

We are returning from the lesser Jihad to the greater Jihad.

Of course, defensive war is permitted only on the condition that the enemies initiate hostilities and raise sword against a weak, defenceless people for having committed the only crime of declaring that God is their Lord. All offensive wars according to Islam are unholy.

Life after Death

The question of life after death has agitated the minds of people belonging to all religions and all ages alike. There is also the atheistic view which totally denies the possibility of life after death. The religions which believe in life after death can be divided into two categories.

❖ Those which believe in the reincarnation of the soul of a dead person into a new human or animal form of existence.
❖ Those which believe in an otherworldly state of existence after death.

The atheistic view is outside the domain of this discussion. As far as Islamic doctrine is concerned, Islam belongs to that category of religions which totally rejects all possibilities of reincarnation in any form. But those who believe in some otherworldly form of spiritual or carnal existence are divided among themselves on so many planes. Within each religion the understanding differs. Hence, with reference to the views held by the followers of various religions, no belief can be attributed to them without fear of contradiction.

In Islam itself there are different views held by different sects or Muslim scholars. The general understanding tends to perceive the otherworldly form as very similar to the carnal one here on earth. The concept of Heaven and Hell consequently present a material image rather than a spiritual image of things to be. Heaven is presented, according to their concept, as an immeasurably large garden literally abounding in beautiful trees casting eternal shadows under which rivers will flow. The rivers would be of milk and honey. The garden will be fruit bearing and all man may desire of fruits would be his at his command. The meat would be that of birds of all sorts; it is only for one to wish which meat he particularly craves. Female companions of exceeding beauty and refinement would be provided to the pious men, with no limit imposed on the number, which will be decided according to their capacity. As many as they can cope with will be theirs. What would they do? How would they relate with each other? Will they bear children or lead a barren life of enjoyment? These are all the moot questions. The enjoyment, as it is conceived, is intensely sensual. No work to be performed, no labour to be wasted, no effort to be made. A perfect life (if such life can be called perfect) of complete and total indolence, with the option of overeating and over-drinking, because also wine will be flowing close to the rivers of milk and honey. No fear of dyspepsia or intoxication! Reclining on heavenly cushions of silk and brocade, they will while their time away in eternal bliss—but what an eternal bliss!

In Islam, there are others who categorically reject this naive understanding of the Quranic references to Heaven, and prove with many a reference to verses of the Holy Quran that what it describes is just metaphorical imagery which has no carnality about it. In fact the Holy Quran makes it amply clear that the form of existence of the life to come will be so different from all known forms of life here on earth, that it is beyond human imagination even to have the slightest glimpse of the otherworldly realities.

$$وَنُنْشِئَكُمْ فِى مَالَاتَعْلَمُونَ$$

We will raise you into a form of which you have not the slightest knowledge. (Quran 56:62)

This is the categorical statement of the Quran on the subject. In recent times, the founder of the Ahmadiyya Community, Hadhrat Mirza Ghulam Ahmad[as] of Qadian, presented this view of spiritual existence as against carnal existence in his unique and outstanding treatise entitled *The Philosophy of the Teachings of Islam*.[5] All views propounded in the book are well documented with Quranic references and traditions of the Holy Founder of Islam. A brief account is reproduced here.

According to his profound study, the life in the hereafter would not be material. Instead, it would be of a spiritual nature of which we can only visualise certain aspects. We cannot determine precisely how things will take shape. One of the salient features of his vision of the hereafter concerns the soul giving birth to another rarer entity, which would occupy the same position in relation to the soul as the soul occupies in relation to our carnal existence here on earth. This birth of a soul from within the soul will be related to the sort of life that we have lived on earth. If our lives here are spent in submission to the will of God and in accordance with His commands, our tastes gradually become cultured and attuned to enjoying spiritual pleasures as against carnal pleasures. Within the soul a sort of embryonic soul begins to take shape. New faculties are born and new tastes are acquired, in which those accustomed to carnal pleasures find no enjoyment. These new types of refined human beings can find the content of their heart. Sacrifice instead of the usurpation of others' rights becomes enjoyable. Forgiveness takes the upper hand of revenge, and love with no selfish motive is born like a second nature,

---

5   *The Philosophy of the Teachings of Islam*, Hadhrat Mirza Ghulam Ahmad, The London Mosque, 1979.

replacing all relationships that have ulterior motives. Thus, one can say a new soul within the soul is in the offing.

All these projections regarding the development of the soul are inferences drawn from various verses of the Holy Quran, yet the exact nature of future events cannot be precisely determined. One can only say that something along these lines would take place, the details of which lie beyond the reach of human understanding.

There are certain aspects of the new life which need to be discussed. The concept of hell and heaven in Islam is completely different from the normally held view. Hell and heaven are not two different places occupying separate time and space. According to the Holy Quran, the heaven covers the entire universe. 'Where would be hell then?' enquired some of the companions of the Holy Prophet[sa]. 'At the same place', was the answer, 'but you do not have the faculty to understand their coexistence.' That is to say in ordinary human terms, they may seem to occupy the same time-space, but in reality because they belong to different dimensions, so they will coexist without interfering and inter-relating with each other.

But what is the meaning of heavenly bliss, the tortures of the fire of hell? In answer to this question, the Promised Messiah[as] has illustrated the issue in the following terms: If a man is almost dying of thirst but is otherwise healthy, cool water can provide him such deeply satisfying pleasure as cannot be derived from the ordinary experience of drinking water, or even the most delicious drink of his choice. If a man is thirsty and hungry as well, and he needs an immediate source of energy, a chilled bunch of grapes can provide him with such deep satisfaction as is not experienced by the same in ordinary circumstances. But the pre-requisite for these pleasures is good health. Now visualise a very sick man, who is nauseating and trying to vomit whatever liquid is left in him and is on the verge of death through dehydration. Offer him a glass of cool water, or a chilled bunch of grapes, then not to mention his accepting them, a mere glance of them would create a state of revulsion and absolute abhorrence in him.

In illustrations like these, the Promised Messiah[as] made it clear that hell and heaven are only issues of relativity. A healthy soul which has acquired the taste for good things, when brought into close proximity of the objects of its choice, will draw even greater pleasure than before. All that a healthy spiritual man was craving was nearness to God and His attributes and to imitate divine virtues. In heaven, such a healthy soul would begin to see and conceive and feel the nearness of the attributes of God like never before. They, according to the Promised Messiah[as] would not remain merely spiritual values, but would acquire ethereal forms and shapes which the newly born heavenly spirit would enjoy with the help of the erstwhile soul which would function as the body. That again would be a matter of relativity. The converse will be true of hell, in the sense that an unhealthy soul would create an unhealthy body for the new soul of the hereafter. And the same factors which provide pleasure to the healthy soul would provide torture and deep suffering for this unhealthy entity.

When we refer to mind or soul in comparison to our carnal body, there is a vast difference in the nature of their existence, which is almost inconceivable. Every part of the body is alive and is throbbing with life, not only in material terms but also in awareness. Every particle of the human body is gifted with some sort of awareness. Scientists try to express that awareness in terms of electronic pulses, but that is a very crude way of describing the overall awareness of the conscious and subconscious mind and the immune system and other independent functions of the human body, which still lie far beyond our power of comprehension.

So what is that awareness? How can it be defined and explained that Ultimate 'I' in every living thing. Can we refer to it as ego in psychological terms? But never has a psychologist succeeded in defining the ego. It is that something which in religious terms is described as the soul. There is no way we can measure the distance between the soul and the carnal body. In terms of rarity the soul, even in our crudest perception, is so rare and ultra-refined that in no way can it be likened to the body that it occupies. Now try to conceive the scenario of the birth of a soul within the soul over a period of billions of years. At the end of a long day we find a soul within a soul which would have the same comparison in terms of rarity as a human soul here on earth has with the human body. Something similar to this will take place and in relative terms the future existence of life would also have two states combined into one entity. In relative terms, one state would be like body and the other like soul. In comparison to our body, our soul would appear like a body to the newly evolved essence of existence.

For further details, readers are advised to read the full treatise, which deals not only with this subject but also discusses some other very interesting topics which agitate the minds of people the world over.

In short, each individual creates his own hell or his own heaven and, in accordance with his own state, each heaven differs from the other person's heaven and each hell differs from the other person's hell, though apparently they occupy the same space and time in otherworldly dimensions.

What happens to man's soul between the time of his carnal death and his resurrection on the Day of Judgement? The Holy Prophet[sa] is reported to have said that after our death windows will open up in the grave; for the pious people windows open from heaven, and for the wicked people they open towards hell. However, if we were to open up a grave we would not find any windows! So literal acceptance of these words will not convey the true meaning of this subject. It is impossible that the Holy Prophet[sa] should ever misinform us; hence here he had to be speaking metaphorically. Had it not been so, then every time we dig up a grave, we should find windows, either opening into hell, or letting in the fragrant and pleasant air of paradise. But we witness neither of these. So what do the Holy Prophet's words mean?

The grave is actually an intermediary phase of existence between this life and the life to come. Here, spiritual life will progress gradually through many stages until it reaches its ultimate destiny. Then by the Command of Allah, a trumpet will be blown and the final spiritual form will come into being. In this interim period, different souls would pass through a semblance of heaven or hell before reaching their final stage of perfection, fit and ready to be raised into a completely transformed entity. The Quran illustrates this concept beautifully:

$$\text{مَا خَلْقُكُمْ وَلَا بَعْثُكُمْ إِلَّا كَنَفْسٍ وَاحِدَةٍ}$$

Your first creation and your second creation will be identical. (Quran 31:29)

Pondering over the birth of a child from a single cell, one finds the following Quranic statement:

هُوَ الَّذِي يُصَوِّرُ كُمْ فِي الْأَرْحَامِ

See how God gives you various shapes in the womb. (Quran 3: 7)

Now this subject is related to the subject of the two identical creations mentioned above. Take for example the case of such children as are congenitally ill. They do not suddenly contract illness at the time of delivery; rather they gradually develop into a state of morbidity which is progressive and which starts from the time of their early embryonic stage. Similarly, the soul of a person who is spiritually diseased, in that embryonic stage before its final resurrection on the Day of Judgement, will suffer through a semblance of hell and will remain uneasy in that period of the grave as does an unhealthy child in the womb of its mother. The ways of a healthy child are totally different, even his kicking is appreciated by the mother.

The question that now arises is: Will the soul also progress as does the child in the mother's womb, and will it passes through all these stages? The answer to this can be found in the very same verse of the Quran: 'Ma khalqukum wa ma ba'sukum illa ka nafsin wahidin —your first creation and your second creation will be identical.

To understand the second creation, we need to understand the way a baby takes shape in a mother's womb. These forms apparently only take nine months to develop, while in reality the creation of life is spread over billions of years. Going back to the beginning of zoological life, the baby passes through almost all the stages of the evolution of life. From the beginning of the pregnancy, through to its culmination nine months later, the development of the child reflects all the stages of creation. In other words, all the phases of evolution are being repeated in those nine months, one after the other, and at such great speed that it is beyond our imagination. It keeps alive the stages of the system of evolution, and presents a picture of it.

The creation of life underwent a long period of development to reach the form that we witness in nine months. This sheds light on the fact that the period of our first creation was very long, and our second creation will also span a long period. By studying these nine months we can learn something of the billions of years of the history of life and also about the evolution of souls in the next world. It is perhaps safe to infer that the time from the early origin of life to the ultimate creation of man would perhaps be needed once again for the development of the soul after the death.

In support of this reasoning, the Quran categorically declares that when the souls are resurrected they will talk to one another, trying to determine how long they tarried on the earth. Some will say, 'We tarried for a day' while others will say, 'For even less than a day.' Allah will then say, 'No even that is not correct.' In other words, Allah will say, 'You tarried on earth for much less than what you estimate.' In reality, the relationship of one life-span to a small part of the day is more or less the same ratio that the time of the soul's resurrection will have to its previous entire life. The further away something is, the smaller it appears. Our childhood seems like an experience of just a few seconds. The greater the distance of the stars, the smaller they appear. What Allah is trying to tell us is that we won't find ourselves being judged the very next day after we die. Instead, judgement will take place in such a distant future that our previous lives will seem like a matter of a few seconds to us, like a small point a long way away.

In short, man's resurrection is described as a transformation that he cannot envisage and an event that is as certain as his existence here on earth. All these subjects have been explained in detail in the Holy Quran.

Predestiny and Free Will

The issue of destiny is a very complicated one, which has been debated through the ages by philosophers and divines alike. In almost every religion there is some reference to the nature of destiny.

We can divide those who believe in destiny into two major categories. Those with the commonly held blind belief in destiny portray it as predetermination by God of everything big and small. This view is popular with some cryptic sects of Sufis (mystics), who live a life apart from the common people. They claim that man has no control over anything. Everything is predetermined. As such all that happens is the unfolding of the grand plan of destiny, known only to God. This is a very problematic concept of the plan of things and inevitably leads to the question of crime and punishment, penalty and reward. If a man has no choice, then there should be neither punishment nor reward for his actions.

The other view is that of free choice, with destiny playing practically no role in whatever man decides and executes.

During the discussion on destiny, another important philosophical issue finds its way into the debate adding further complications, and that is the question of pre-cognition. What does the pre-knowledge of God have to do with the things to come? That is the question, the answer to which has been rather poorly handled by both parties in the debate. We do not propose to enter into a lengthy review of the comparative merits of the arguments of the believers and unbelievers of destiny, but would only attempt to portray the Islamic viewpoint.

Destiny has many categories, each playing a distinct role in their respective spheres of operation, working simultaneously. The laws of nature reign supreme and none is above the influence of them. This is the general plan of things which can be referred to as the widest concept of destiny. Whoever follows the laws of nature with a profound understanding of them will gain some advantage over others who do not. Such people are always destined to benefit and to shape a better life for themselves. But none of them is predestined to belong to any specific grouping in relation to their being on the right or wrong side of the laws of nature.

There was a time in the era just preceding the Renaissance in Europe, when the Muslim world of the orient was far more advanced in its understanding of the laws of nature. The Muslims consequently were in a position to draw benefits attendant upon this knowledge. When, later on, this unprejudiced and open minded study of nature shifted to the West, it ushered in a new day of light of knowledge for the West while the East began to plunge into a long, dark night of wishful thinking, superstition and dreaming. This is destiny of course, but of a different type. The only law which is predetermined in relation to this destiny is the unchangeable command that whoever studies nature without prejudices, and permits himself to be led to wherever the laws of nature would lead him, he would tread the path of eternal progress. This is the general and all-pervasive category of destiny which transcends everything, except the laws of destiny relating to religion.

Before taking up the discussion of destiny in application to religion, we should further explore some areas of this universal destiny of the laws of nature. In their larger global applications, they exhibit some features of predetermination but of a different type than commonly understood. In this sense we are speaking of such seasonal or periodic changes in atmospheric balances which represent a very complicated eco-system in which even distant events such as sun spots play a role. Similarly, the meteoric invasions of planets bring about certain changes, which are reflected upon the earth through corresponding variations in weathers, climates etc. These larger influences, together with periodic alterations in climates (which are caused by various factors many of which are as yet undetermined), sometimes bring about subtle changes in the growth patterns of vegetative and animal life on earth. Again there are factors responsible for droughts or shifting of seasons from one part of the earth to another. Ice-ages and global warming, in alternation, are but some consequences of various cosmic influences. However, these larger influences do not specifically affect an individual's life on earth, but in the final analysis, as individuals are all members of the Homo-Sapiens family, they are affected to a degree.

There is no evidence to indicate that each man's life is pre-ordained, and that he has no choice or option in choosing between good and bad, right and wrong. The Holy Quran categorically rejects the concept of compulsion, and clearly states that every human being is free to choose between good and evil:

لَآ إِكْرَاهَ فِى الدِّينِ

There shall be no compulsion in matters of faith. (Quran 2:257)

And:

لَا يُكَلِّفُ اللَّهُ نَفْسًا إِلَّا وُسْعَهَا لَهَا مَا كَسَبَتْ وَعَلَيْهَا مَا اكْتَسَبَتْ

Allah burdens not any soul beyond its capacity. It shall have the reward it earns, and it shall get the punishment it incurs. (Quran 2:287)

And again:

وَأَنْ لَيْسَ لِلْإِنْسَانِ إِلَّا مَا سَعَى

And that man will have nothing but what he strives for. (Quran 53:40)

However, in relation to religion, there are some spheres of destiny which are predetermined and unchangeable. They are referred to in the Holy Quran as the *Sunnah* of God. One such Sunnah is the destiny that God's messengers will always be victorious, whether they are accepted or not. If they are rejected, it is the opponents whose designs are frustrated. The prophets, their messages and mission must always prevail, regardless of how powerful their enemies may be a few examples in the living history of man are the confrontations between Moses[as] and Pharoah, between Jesus[as] and his opponents, and between Muhammad[sa] and his adversaries. The triumph of religion is what remains as the legacy of past struggles between prophets and their adversaries. Abraham[as] and his faith, and those who uphold him and his message, predominate the world. Moses[as] and those who revere him, Jesus[as] and his message, and the Prophet Muhammad[sa] and what he stood for, almost dominate the entire world. But none is found today who uphold the cause and values of their opponents. This destiny does not come into play in other confrontations between men and men. The general rule there is that the strong will annihilate the weak. In religious destiny, it is the converse which becomes an inviolable principle.

Although the laws of nature run a smooth course and one does not normally find exceptions to the general rules, but according to the plan of things inferred from various verses of the Quran, the laws of nature known to us belong to many categories and spheres. They do not clash with each other within their spheres, but when they stand at cross-purpose with other laws, the laws which possess greater force always prevail over the weaker ones. Even a law of the widest and farthest influence can be defeated within a small sphere by a more powerful one operating against it. Thermodynamic and electromagnetic laws in opposition to the laws of gravitation can win in limited areas of influence. However, the gravitational law is much wider in its influence, and more far-reaching. As man's understanding of nature develops from age to age, things which would have been rejected as impossible are becoming conceivable and matters of commonplace observation.

In view of this introduction, according to Islam, if God decides to favour a special servant of His with a special manifestation of some hidden laws, such manifestations are regarded by the onlookers as miracles and supernatural events. But these things happen in accordance with the laws of nature, which are subtly controlled to bring about an amazing effect. Here, destiny plays a specific role in the life of a special servant of God.

Similarly, destiny can also be understood in relation to the genetic, social, economic or educational background of the individual, who seems to be a helpless product of circumstances. This helplessness of the individual makes his destiny, over which he has no control. Thus it is said that a rich man's child is born with a silver spoon in his mouth.

The circumstances in which a person is born, the society in which he is reared, the day-to-day game of chance which plays a role in everybody's life, the strikes of so-called luck in favour or against one, the accidents which one may escape or fall prey to, are all areas where the individual has very little choice. Yet it may not be assumed that he was particularly targeted for such events or accidents which play an important role in the making or unmaking of his life.

Individuals who are born in homes riddled with poverty are far more likely to fall prey to petty or even serious crimes. Poverty is the most compulsive force of all factors which create and promote crime. If this is understood to be destiny, then it will cast a grave reflection on the Creator. So, first of all it should be clearly understood that destiny is only part of a grand scheme of things which does not issue particular edicts against people in particular families. In a larger economic plan, there are bound to be more fortunate and less fortunate people with relative advantages and disadvantages. It is wrong to say that they were individually stamped by a maker of destiny, even before their births, to be born under certain specific circumstances. Yet there are other questions to be answered. How would they be treated in relation to the crimes committed by them as against those who are born in comparatively healthier circumstances, and who have very few, if any, background factors to egg them onto crime? If the crime is the same, shall they be treated alike? The Holy Quran answers this intricate question in the following verse:

لَا يُكَلِّفُ اللَّهُ نَفْسًا إِلَّا وُسْعَهَا

No soul will be burdened beyond its capacity. (Quran 2:287)

This means that background factors, social and other, that surround a person, will certainly be taken into account, and he will be judged accordingly. In the sight of Allah, it is not just the crime itself which is mechanically punished, but all factors which go into the making of the crime are also brought into consideration, with the ultimate result that justice will be done. The fortunate and the unfortunate will not be judged with equal severity and, most certainly, license will be given to the environment and the background of a person who commits crime. Likewise, acts of goodness will be rewarded far more in the case of a man whose circumstances are likely to discourage him from doing good, than a man whose environment is one in which acts of goodness are taken for granted.

Thus the issue of destiny is highly complicated, but as the ultimate decision lies in the hands of the All-Knowing, All-Beneficent, All-Powerful and All-Wise God, in the final analysis, the dictates of justice will indeed prevail.

There are certain areas in which man is free to exercise his will, where he can choose between good or bad, right or wrong, and for which he will be held responsible. On the other hand, there are areas in which man has little choice of his own, and appears to be a pawn in the hand of the mover. The general plan of things in nature, which covers and controls the destinies of nations and peoples, is one such area. The circumstances of a wider application make an individual of society completely helpless; he has no choice but to move along like a straw being carried by the waves of a river in spate.

The subject of destiny is a very complicated and vast one and requires a separate and fuller treatment. So, with these few hints, we would like to bring this discussion to an end.

Conclusion

We draw the attention of the audience to a grave injustice done to Islam by the Western world. As has been well demonstrated, with reference to the teachings of the Quran and the injunctions of the Holy Prophet[sa], Islam can only be described as a religion of peace. It covers all aspects of human life and delivers a message of peace to its adherents in their relationship to fellow human beings as well as in their relationship to God. Without prejudice or fear of contradiction, we can assert that no other religion emphasises peace even a part as much as Islam does. Although followers of many religions do make similar claims, here we are talking of a claim which should be fully supported by injunctions contained in the divine scriptures. If however, every religion emphasises to the same degree the role of peace in human affairs, it is a most welcome gesture, which we do appreciate, and on which one can build hope for the future of mankind. In that case, it should be the prime responsibility of the religious leadership of all religions of the world to bring out the precious message of peace so much needed by mankind today.

Tragically however, even the adherents of Islam present it as a threat to international peace by promoting terrorism in the name of God and in the name of the Holy Prophet[sa] of Islam, who was a living paragon of peace. If the West presents Islam as a religion of terror and denial of fundamental human rights, the fault is not entirely theirs. It is largely shared, to say the least, by the clergy of various Muslim denominations. To talk of religious supremacy in all other areas of human interest and to maintain at the same time that Islam emphatically denies the internationally accepted concept of human rights, is enough in itself to blemish the image of Islam.

Irrespective of whether the divine scriptures of other religions have presented the ideal of universal peace or not, it can be said without fear of contradiction that all religions seem to be inclined to such an ideal. This lays the foundation for a concerted effort on the part of the religious leaders of the world to work jointly for global peace. Instead of playing up our differences, it would be far more advisable and advantageous if the religious leadership highlighted points of agreement. This, we are certain would be accepted as the binding factors between all religious denominations. Consequently, it could lead to the bringing together of the entire human race, regardless of country, creed or colour. If religions do not undertake this work none else can, because this is the only force capable of transcending national, geographic and racial barriers.

With this earnest appeal to the leadership of the world religions, we bring this short treatise to a close, hoping for the best. The quest for peace is a matter of human survival, and as such should not be taken lightly.

Index

E

Einstein, 9
embryonic development, 55
   Quranic verses about, 55
equality, 9
evolution, 56

F

fasting, 43
   importance of, 45
   Islamic method of, 44
   method of, 45
   Muhammad[sa] on the limits
     of, 45
   obligatory type of, 43
   voluntary type of, 45
free will, 57
   Quranic verses about, 59, 60

G

God
   all prophets taught the
     Unity of, 18
   Angels in relation to, 11
   declaration of Unity of, 8
   does not need prayer, 33
   emulating the attributes of,
     34, 52
   improving one's relationship
     with, 32, 34

   misconceptions about, 16
   sends prophets, 28
   the *Sunnah* of, 60
   Unity of, 41
   Unity of, 7, 9, 16

H

Hajj, 40
   method of performing, 42
Heaven, 54
   differing views on, 48
   Islamic concept of, 49, 51
   location of, 51
   Mirza Ghulam Ahmad[as] on,
     51
Hell, 54
   differing views on, 48
   Islamic concept of, 51
   location of, 51
   Mirza Ghulam Ahmad[as] on,
     51
Holy Books, 6
   Old and New Testaments, 16
   reconciling contradictions
     in, 16, 19
   truth of all, 25
   two categories of, 21
   understanding the context
     of, 22, 23
Holy Ghost, 11
Holy War
   definition of jihad, 47
   Muhammad[sa] on, 47

Quranic verses about, 47
types of, 47

I

Imam, 35
Ishmael[as], 41
Islam, 64
  and the West, 64
  Articles of Faith of, 5
  belief in all prophets, 27
  meaning of, 5
  unifies all the religions, 18

J

Jesus[as], 27, 60
  miracles of, 29
  understanding the teachings
    of, 23
Jihad. *See* Holy War
Judgement Day. *See* Day of
    Judgement
justice
  Quranic verses about, 62

K

Krishna, 15, 25, 26, 27
  Muhammad[sa] on, 25

L

life
  the creation of, 56
Life after Death, 48
  differing views on, 48
  Islamic concept of, 50
  Mirza Ghulam Ahmad[as] on,
    50
  Muhammad[sa] on, 54
  Quranic verses about, 49

M

Mecca, 41
miracles
  Islamic concept of, 61
Moses[as], 27, 60
mosques, 38
Muhammad[sa], 60
  and the Angel Gabriel, 13
  miracles of, 30
  on God and prayer, 33
  on Holy War, 47
  on Krishna, 25
  on Life after Death, 54
  on the limits of fasting, 45
  on the location of Heaven
    and Hell, 51
  status of, 28, 31

N

nature
  and destiny, 58
  harmony in, 61
  Muslim understanding of, 58

P

Pilgrimage. *See* Hajj
polytheism, 17
poverty, 62
prayer, 32
  contents of, 38
  in congregation, 35
  in private, 38
  meaning of, 34
  purpose of, 33
  Quranic verse about, 34
  role of mosques in, 38
  the method of, 36
  two types of, 38
predestiny. *See* destiny
Promised Messiah. *See* Ahmad,
    Mirza Ghulam[as]
prophethood, 29
  finality of, 31
  Quranic verses about, 30
  Quranic verses about the
    continuation of, 31
prophets, 6, 23
  categories of teachings of, 32
  come from God, 28
  inevitable success of, 60

Islamic belief in all, 27
non-Arab, 24
taught the Unity of God, 18

Q

Quran, 31
  on Angels, 14
  on common religious
    teachings, 18
  on embryonic development,
    55
  on free will, 59, 60
  on harmony in creation, 9
  on Holy War, 47
  on justice, 62
  on Life after Death, 49
  on prophethood, 30
  on the continuation of
    prophethood, 31
  on the need of God for
    prayer, 33
  on the purpose of prayer, 34
  on the Resurrection, 54
  scientific facts in the, 20
  universal nature of the, 20

R

Ramadhan, 44, 46
reincarnation, 48
religion
  means of unification of, 18

Quranic verse about, 18
Resurrection, 55
   Quranic verses about the, 54

S

Safa and Marwah, 41
Satan, 15
science. Also see *embryonic
   development*
   Quranic verses relating to,
     20
soul, 12, 52
   definition of the, 53
   development of the, 55
   evolution of the, 56
   period until the resurrection
     of the, 54, 56
   the effect of prayer on the,
     35
Spain, 4
spending in the cause of Allah,
   39

T

Torah, 22

U

Unity of God, 5, 6, 16
   as taught by all prophets, 18
   declaration of, 8
   with respect to creation, 9
   with respect to human
     actions, 7
   with respect to unity of
     mankind, 9, 10, 41

V

Vedas, 21

W

West, the, 64
   Islam and, 64
world peace, 64
worship. *See* prayer

Z

Zakat. *See* spending in the cause
   of Allah
Zoroaster, 26